Love Holds You is a hymn to the soul's journey. Though the poet "builds a bonfire from all the old maps," she has drawn a new one here for the reader, charting a path through beauty and heartbreak to the realm beyond "the country of certainty." Each poem is a summons to reverence, be it in a hospital hallway, at a gravesite, or on a bed of "moss and mulch." This is as much a prayerbook as a poetry offering. May you find sanctuary among these pages, and a mirror for your soul.

—Kim Rosen,
author of *Saved by a Poem: The Transformative Power of Words*

This is a wonderful, generous, gentle book. Read these poems slowly . . . let them permeate into your day and make it richer . . . or read them—like me in a rush of tears and smiles—and gratitude to Christine Valters Paintner for reminding us that poetry allows us to soar above the world, to dig deep beneath it, and just to simply, profoundly be in it.

—Clare Shaw,
poet and author of *Flood*, *Straight Ahead*, and *Head On*

POEMS AND
DEVOTIONS
FOR TIMES OF
UNCERTAINTY

Love
Holds
You

CHRISTINE
VALTERS
PAINTNER

IRON
PEN

PARACLETE PRESS
BREWSTER, MASSACHUSETTS

2023 First Printing

Love Holds You: Poems and Devotions for Times of Uncertainty

Copyright © 2023 by Christine Valters Paintner

ISBN 978-1-64060-732-3

The Iron Pen name and logo are trademarks of Paraclete Press.

Library of Congress Cataloging-in-Publication data
Names: Paintner, Christine Valters, author.
Title: Love holds you : poems and devotions for times of uncertainty
   Christine Valters Paintner.
Description: Brewster, Massachusetts : Iron Pen, 2022. | Summary: "From
   Christine Valters Paintner comes poetry and meditations on the many ways
   love comes into our lives, to help in dark and troubled times"--
   Provided by publisher.
Identifiers: LCCN 2022029646 (print) | LCCN 2022029647 (ebook) | ISBN
   9781640607323 (trade paperback) | ISBN 9781640607347 (pdf) | ISBN
   9781640607330 (epub)
Subjects: BISAC: POETRY / Subjects & Themes / Inspirational & Religious |
   POETRY / Subjects & Themes / Death, Grief, Loss | LCGFT: Poetry.
Classification: LCC PS3616.A337848 L68 2022 (print) | LCC PS3616.A337848
   (ebook) | DDC 811/.6--dc23/eng/20220628
LC record available at https://lccn.loc.gov/2022029646
LC ebook record available at https://lccn.loc.gov/2022029647

10 9 8 7 6 5 4 3 2 1

Published by Paraclete Press

Brewster, Massachusetts

www.paracletepress.com

Printed in India

Contents

Love's Seeking and Finding

The Love of the Ancestors

The Love of the Mystics

Closing

Introduction

Most of these poems were written during the time of pandemic. The call to compassionate retreating came naturally for my strong hermit side. I found myself, rather than getting bored with home, falling more in love with the mundane aspects of my life: the boxes on our patio growing herbs, the way my favorite chair has shaped itself to my body, my dog's daily eagerness for walks and cuddles. As I lingered more than usual I found deep appreciation for the radical ordinariness of my days.

In the heart of a season filled with anxieties around personal health and well-being, around economic impact, around tremendous collective grief and loss, I found that there was one thing I wanted to remember daily: my prayers were calling me back to the ground of love that I believe undergirds us all. This isn't always easy to remember, and sometimes reading the news I question whether it is even true. Writing poems about love became an act of cultivating trust. The moments that trust dissolved, I would pick up my pen and try and remember what I loved or how love had been made visible to me that day.

Most of these poems are not directly about the pandemic per se. They are love poems that arose out of a desire to pay close attention when things seemed to be falling apart and to name what it was that endures. Many of the poems are dream-like settings, where a new reality erupts into the everyday.

Love doesn't make our struggles vanish. It doesn't mean carrying perpetual optimism into our days or even having to believe that everything will be okay. Those things are not seductive for me in a world when so many have so much to grieve. It does mean that I believe Love is the foundation of everything and holds us in our sorrow as well as our delight. This is in large part why I write poems, to hold this tension of living in a world that can be so devasting and also so staggeringly beautiful.

Origins

If I could peer far enough down
a robin's pulsing throat, would I see
notes piled there waiting to be flung
into freshness of morning?

If I close my eyes and burrow
my face into peony's petals,
would I discover the source
of its scent, a sacred offering?

Can I plunge inside
and find a lifetime of words
spooled tightly inside my heart
ready for a tug?

If I dig beneath the bedrock
will I find love there,
solid like iron or does it flow like magma
filling in all of the empty spaces?

What happens when you stop and gaze with loving wonder
upon some simple, quiet, and unadorned element of nature
that throws itself into the wild world, and you are the lucky
recipient present to witness it into being?

Love is at the foundation of all I do or am.
There is no place empty of love.

I Begin

The sheets hang white on the line.
    They billow like sails.
    I dream of the ocean.

The garden bed cleared out
    for winter. Dark soil waits.
    I dream of snowdrops.

The cup sits on the counter.
    A hungry mouth wide open.
    I dream of tea with you.

Sheets, dirt, cup.
    Indifferent to my desire.
    My pen hovers, casting a shadow
    on the page.

What happens when you look upon the ordinary tools of your daily life as holy vessels? What other holy vessels evoke a sense of the sacred for you??

Everything in my life can point me to something bigger, more expansive.

How to Pray

Attune your ears to the murmurs
of bugs and birds, whispers
of seeds carried on the breeze.

Place your hands either side
of the dog's warm head,
breathe with its animal body.

Let your feet guide the way
each day, while trees
track seasons.

Remind your body how it says yes
to blossom, fruit, release, and rest,
each its own kind of prayer.

Notice how you tremble
at seeing the moon hover,
as you steep in its opal glow,

knowing your prayer is sometimes
a quiet longing in darkness,
some nights a long howl.

What aliveness calls you to prayer?
What ordinary moments inspire devotion in you?

My senses are portals to the sacred manifestations in this world
always present and available. I open my heart and discover the
world calls me to bow down in adoration.

Living in
Tension

At the end of the Introduction I shared that I write poems to hold the tension of "living in a world that can be so devasting and also so staggeringly beautiful." This is in large part why the mystic's path calls to me so clearly. In the space beyond words and thoughts, I can rest into the reality of our humanity. I can bear witness to the violence and to the stunning acts of compassion. It isn't like measuring the balance on a scale, it is more of a way of being with these truths.

The second poem in this section, "In a Dark Time," emerged near the start of the pandemic. Everything was so unknown, there was so much suffering. Our task in the world as artists and pilgrims, as spiritual seekers, is not to deny the pain we see but to add our own cries of lament to the collective. There are too many superficial platitudes thrown around carelessly by "spiritual" people. Love calls us to be with the sorrow, to journey with the brokenhearted and not try to fix their pain. Love asks that we bear witness, that we open our eyes to see.

Poetry can help us in times of disorientation. A word or line finds us and carries us forward in the midst of unknowing. Sometimes we have to let all the old ways of navigating our lives fall away. Maps carry us only so far.

The poems in this section are my effort to create a space where we can linger in that place between where we can't reconcile the bodies piling up from war or illness with the unfolding of the first pink rose of spring. We can only grieve and celebrate. We can only breathe and feel and be.

When All Feels Lost

The map is not the territory
—Alfred Korzybski

All the old signposts have fallen,
wood cracked and rotted,
atlases crumble, a pile of maps
flutter and dart like hummingbird
wings, the GPS signal is out of range.

Her compass slips from her hand,
the only thing she knows is that
she walks in circles now,
the trees ahead familiar
but really nothing is the same.
She wanders for hours, days,
weeks, loses track of the nights
as one tumbles into another.

Finally, she stops, builds
a bonfire from all the old maps
still in her pack, invites others
who wander by to gather,
each of them savors warmth
from flame and kindness,
laughs while they tell stories
of how they once knew the way.

Her eyes meet another,
hand outstretched, together
their breath rises in white spirals
into cold air and they
stay still long enough
to learn to love the quiet ache,
the old longing to be sure,
to see the country of certainty
as a memory receding
like an evening horizon until
there is only the black bowl of sky.

They begin to hear the whisper
of breezes, the secrets of birds,
follow the underground stream
that runs through each of them,
and they no longer ask
which way to go,
but sit and savor this
together, under night sky
illumined by fire and stars.

What are the maps and compasses of your life that
you cling to? How might getting lost be
a way to find yourself again?

I rest under a vast night sky, learning to trust in waiting and
watching. Unknowing and mystery become close companions.

In a Dark Time

Do not rush to make meaning.
When you smile and tell me what purpose
this all serves, you deny grief
a room inside you,
you turn from thousands who cross
into the Great Night alone,
from mourners aching to press
one last time against the warm
flesh of their beloved,
from the wailing that echoes
in the empty room.

When you proclaim who caused this,
I ask you to pause, rest in the dark silence
first before you contort your words
to fill the hollowed-out spaces,
remember the soil will one day
receive you back too.
Sit where sense has vanished,
control has slipped away,
with futures unraveled,
where every drink tastes bitter
despite our thirst.

When you wish to give a name
to that which haunts us,
you are refusing to sit
with the woman who walks
the hospital hallway and hears
the beeping stop again and again,
to be with the man perched on a bridge
over the rushing river.
Do not let your handful of light
sting the eyes of those
who have bathed in darkness.

Can you sit in the quiet darkness?
What are the experiences that prompt you to reach
for the light too quickly?

I allow darkness to hold me. I don't rush to figure out
what it all means.

Field Notes on Love

1. It begins in the body, a laying down of armor

2. Looking up at treetops and the space they give to one another

3. The dog pressed against me each morning

4. The meadow where the rumpus of wildflowers sway together

5. How I wrote to my father to tell him we could no longer speak

6. I later moved to the city where he is buried

7. The way the ripe pear loosens itself from the branch

8. My return to you after separating because I knew what it was to be cherished

9. Renewing our vows in a stony rain-soaked field

10. Your warm hand holding mine as we left the hospital and walked out into snow

What field notes would you add in your own
explorations of love's presence?

I find love in both the quiet moments as well as the times when
my world felt like it was crumbling. I think of the way that all
of creation offered itself to me.

Rise and Fall

The tide can't wash away
the jubilant sparrow
outside my window
or the urgency of seeds
erupting in green generosity.

It can't flood away
my memory of your hands
how impossibly
soft they were even as your body
turned rigid, let go.

The tide can't erase my love
for rainy days, how dark earth
soaks, clouds break apart
like curtains on the opening act
and everything gleams
when sun's glow re-emerges.

The tide can't wash away
my love for this world,
only remind me how everything
rises and recedes,
treasures embedded in wet sand,
smoothed by time and brine.

What wisdom do the tides have for you? What is the rising and receding of your own life right now?

When the tide ebbs I wander the shoreline looking for gifts.
When the tide flows I swim in the sea's embrace.

Offering

I am not director or conductor,
I am the field wide and green,
I am the sea rising,
claiming shore for myself,
now receding to reveal
what is hidden.

This hunger matters,
I dare not starve myself
any longer. Set the table, the feast
already awaits. No matter how much
I eat, the banquet is always piled
with fruit, honey dripping from bowls,
the wine glass full.

What are the things in your life you want to direct or conduct?
What longing is rising from your depths, begging you to
nourish it with sustenance for your soul?

I savor the feast whenever it is set before me.

So Much is Ending

Fruit lies in piles around trees,
a slush of waning nectar,
can I love that which has
moved past ripeness?
That which heaps itself
in sticky-scented rot?
Can I love the mottled skin,
petals tumbling to ground,
sharp wind shaking loose
the clutch of leaves?
Can I love what could have been,
promises unfulfilled?
Destiny unclaimed?
Can the current of regret
carry me to old shores?
Will I look in the mirror
at my scars and lines
and see a ragged map?
Will I linger a while,
re-reading the final page?

This is a poem of questions already. What is your relationship to endings? What tales of regret do you carry through your days? Is it time to bless them with a healing embrace, releasing them to the past that couldn't be, yet all the time creating the matrix of this present moment where you now stand?

I embrace the end as a doorway to new beginnings.

Sometimes

Sometimes I awake
and read the news,

and want to hold the world
as far away as possible.

Sometimes I walk
in the quiet woods

and I want to draw
that vibrant green

as close as I can,
to embrace it

and be embraced.
This is the dance of my life,

a repulsion,
a falling in love.

Can you be gentle with the push and pull of your heart holding
both like a musical score which sings the song of your life?

I make room within myself for the full spectrum of my being.

Vision

Each morning
I walk the canal
alert for heron

in her stillness
all wing and air,
gray parade of feather

revealing what I
have suspected
all this time,

that beauty arrives
when the heart is open,
and for a moment

my grief for the world
is suspended, held aloft
by light and breeze,

lifted like the sun
each day, an orb
sailing across the horizon.

When you walk in the world is there a bird, insect, or beast
that helps to lift your heart?

I offer my grief over to nature, allowing it to be held.

Rising

I must know the voice of mountain,
how she rises and rises toward sky,
her body a prayer of endurance.

I must know the sounds of wind
carving, refining stone
for a million years.

I must know the howling peaks,
glaciers, eruptions, frictions,
collisions which brought her here.

I am rising too, cool ascent, hawk
circling, feathers brush sky and stone.
I am also descending, resting

in her cool shadows,
embrace of granite, quartz,
limestone bones of earth.

I listen to streams of gold
running through her great gashed
heart, the steadiness of time

and its tumult, asking me
to spread wide my aching wings
assent to this summons

in the only way I can,
asking how committed I really am,
asking how long I will persist.

Have you listened to the voice of the mountain lately?
To the sounds of wind? To the longing in your wings?

I say yes to the wild call arising in my heart. I commit.
I will endure.

Circles

On mornings when I gaze
across a sunlit lake
all blue and foam and shimmer

I barely see the cracking edges,
how this world is crumbling
and I am forever falling apart,

forever coming together again.

I walk across the meadow,
grass trampled under my feet
only to spring upright again,

this resilience its own kind of prayer.

How my animal body knows
the earth-scented, green-growing
freshness, the place of blooming

as a place inside,
how it wants to run through fields
as if everything is possible,

a golden sea of grass and blossom,
tiny globes of wonder as dew
magnifies light and color,

thrumming of bee and cricket,
how it knows one day this earth
will be upturned, soil giving way
to welcome me back home.

*Where in your life have you noticed the gap between the
crumbling contours and the eternal refashioning of your inner
self, that constant flux of forming, dying, re-forming, the
sacred gift of resilience which is your deepest prayer
tenderly holding your fragile life?*

*I make space for my own falling apart and my coming back
together again. I honor the many circles life offers to me.*

A Forest of Desire

I walk the soft earth
and the trees announce
my presence to one another,
knowing I have come here
to listen, to bow down, to touch
the soil that will one day
embrace my body again.

They know how much I long
to sleep on moss and mulch,
to dream of greening. They hear
my grief at this world,
so lost, so full
of coldness and beauty.

When I leave the forest,
she remembers me,
the space I inhabited
briefly vibrates
with longing and loneliness,
awaiting my return.

Do you have a forest, woodland, or special tree you like to connect with? What landscape delineates the contours of your soul, making your spirit shiver in time with the field of grasses which hold the memory of your presence tenderly until you return?

I bring the weight of my heart to the greening world and let myself be held.

Evening Arrives at the Lake

Even endings have beginnings
when the sun glides behind branches
black stencil on gold leaf
clouds form pink piles on the horizon
crows gather, feathered muscles
flexing in the trees,
raucous caws fill the air
crying down a curtain of dark
which drapes over everything.

The moon rises mottled and delicate
reflects in the water below
and anyone paying attention can see
how darkness holds open
its round white mouth
getting ready to sing.

When was the last time you sat present for the arrival of evening? Witnessed the changing colors, growing darkness, and rising moon? What song does sunset sing to you?

I embrace the gifts and beauty that endings bring, knowing that the seeds of new beginnings are held there as well.

Autumn Field Notes

The marigold stands with a single yellow petal.

The leaf, half green, half red, curls in on itself.

The mouse races across the path, trying
     to outrun the coming cold.

The old sycamore leans and sighs.

The spiderweb trembles under the weight
     of several flies.

The amber light slides down from the sun.

The swifts who darted all summer like tiny acrobats,
     leave behind only the sound of wind
     rushing through an empty sky.

*When you imagine the season of autumn, what
are your own field notes or observances of color,
sound, and sensation? How do the echoes of autumn
reverberate through the landscape of your soul?*

*I greet the world and listen for what the season
has to offer me as wisdom.*

Where Love Lives

The sun is a shy lemon
peeking from behind a curtain
before disappearing.

All I want to do is lift away,
live in that weightless place
where gravity has no claim on me,
where lightness is my name.

All I want to do is bend back down
into dust and mud, savor how stones
absorb sunlight and become radiant,
until heaviness is my name.

I see that I am always both:
I am stone, weight, gravity.
I am angel, feathered, floating.
Love lives in the wonder
of the in-between, the longing
for all possible worlds,
the way sunlight explodes
its lemon tartness in my mouth,
the way sunlight lingers
at the heart of every stone.

*What are the moments of life that stir you to a longing to fly
away, feel lightness? What are the moments that prompt you to
desire the density of things, to know the world as solid?
Have you found the gateway into the world of divine
longing where weight and weightlessness merge in the
interior landscape of your soul?*

*I am both weightless and heaviness, both feather and
stone. I hold contradictions within myself.*

Midlife

I am in the October of my life
when the great golden light
reveals treasures.
The branches are heavy with fruit, so full
of juice and sweetness
ready to break open between
teeth and tongue, nourish me
before the winds come and strip
everything bare in one sudden gust.

I am not there yet. I know to bask
in the glow of maple and ginkgo's
glorious turning,
to hold my arms open
gathering pears and plums,
ready to one day ride
the wild wind home.

What season of life are you in right now?
How does the natural world reflect this back to you?
What treasures are revealing themselves to you?

*I let go of my hold on things no longer needed. I practice
each day with hands open, ready to receive new gifts.*

Possibility of Angels

If they do exist, I hope they're
not cherubs with pudgy baby bodies
and tiny faltering wings.

I want my angels large and solid,
able to carve stone with the wind
from their wings.

I want them to be filled
with the heaviness of longing,
to know what it is

to have to eat your heart
for breakfast just to survive.
Might they appear

like Gabriel before Mary
asking the hard questions,
asking you to consent to darkness.

Have you ever had an encounter with an angel? What do angels look like in your imagination? If an angel were to appear before you now, what hard question might they ask you to consent to?

I trust that there are presences in the world here to hold me in loving support.

Patient

My head is full of iron filings. The bed is a magnet.
The green light flickers above. The scent of bleach
fills my nose. The nurse enters and leaves the room
like a cuckoo bird on an old clock, chirping each time.
I hear the fluorescents buzz. They want to tell me
a secret. I try to decipher the pattern. A water spot
on the ceiling takes a hundred different shapes
like a dark cloud on a windy day.

Once a day the doctor enters, arms flailing,
a conductor with his orchestra of interns
nodding their heads, scribbling on clipboards.
They rush out of the room before
they hear the sound the lights whisper
or see the way the shape on the ceiling
has shifted once again.

Have you ever experienced a debilitating illness from whose clutches you could only lie back and look, and keep looking until visions of things never before noticed seem to suddenly insinuate themselves into your life? Does the memory of this make you wonder about a world you forever pass without seeing?

Those times when my body asks me to slow down, rest, and recover, I say yes knowing this too is an act of love.

A Letter to My Adolescent Self

"listen I love you joy is coming"
—Kim Addonizio

Listen, I know life right now
feels like heartache
is your mother tongue,
parents who live in the shadows,
you stumbling down
the dark corridors of youth
trying all the locked doors
and knobs breaking off in your hands.

I won't promise this heartache ends.
You'll lose people you love: death, betrayal,
a slow fade. Some will dissolve
like salt on the tongue. There will be moments
you're sure you are drowning, arms flailing,

but sometimes your frantic waving
will summon a joy you never knew could exist
arriving like an elephant emerging
from a still forest or a hatching egg placed
in your palm, and you will know delight
is not an afterthought, nor a luxury,

but an amaryllis opening the first petal,
its red tongue whispering secrets
of all the loves it has ever known.

What advice do you have for your younger self?
If you could whisper in their ear across time,
what do you want them to know?

I open my heart to joy today by paying attention to small
miracles. I send this joy back to myself in those moments of
heartbreak and painful uncertainty.

At the End of Time

You never imagined
how tedious the apocalypse
would be, its long days of waiting,
like an endless gray carpet
unrolling in front of you.

And yet the dog still begs
for breakfast and there are her piles
to pick up in the yard, the bills to pay,
all your loved ones' faces
now framed by a screen.

When a friend becomes ill
you taste fear like a bitter root
stuck in your throat, a wedge
of granite in your stomach.

This morning you saw the heron
standing motionless at the river's edge
and you think perhaps
you had been a heron once.
Her absolute stillness,
how she waits without complaint,
watches while the water rushes by her,
endless. And the moment that silver

flashes in the river, her direct aim,
how she savors what shimmers
in her mouth like tasting
the tiniest morsel of truth.

During your own moments of waiting, of struggle,
of unknowing, what have been the small signs
of a deeper truth abiding in the world?

I make time to walk today and to look closely
at the world around me, listening for what
she might want to reveal.

Waning and Waxing

The moon sings her prayers nightly,
breathing in, her belly fills with light.

Breathing out,
she becomes a sliver.

The stars stand waiting at the mouth
of her cave, but she slips out silently

back into the night.
Those same stars write ancient blessings

across the black parchment
of sky. Most of them have died

a thousand years ago and yet their light
still pulses and throbs,

for all those who have known
what it is to fade into nothing

only to awaken one day with a song
we just can't stop singing.

What is your relationship to the moon's phases?
How do her cycles of expansion and contraction reveal
something to you about your own life?

I breathe in and welcome the waxing of my heart. I
breathe out and embrace the waning of my soul.

After the Storm

The year I turned forty
I flew 5000 miles to walk
cobblestone streets alone,
time to think and be
in a season of grief,
and there I came close
to death, a clot in my leg and lung.

The city was buried in snow
and I was alive. How grateful
I felt! How I knew it could have been
otherwise, the world
both more intense and ghostly
all at once. I pressed my body
against a dark doorway
and turned back defiant.
There were no flashing lights
showing me the way, no urgency,
just a quiet knowing, a trust
in my body's fierceness.

Two years later I uprooted
my whole life to walk those
same cobblestones daily, I felt
no need to seize anything or suck
the marrow from life's bones
as Thoreau once counseled,
rather I wanted to receive it all
slowly,

like the bird who gathers
discarded things to create a nest,
like waiting for the first
petal to drop,
like water dripping from icicles
after the storm.

Have you ever had an experience of coming close to your own death? What was the impact on your life? And if not, can you imagine this experience and what it might urge you toward?

I attend to the daily graces of life, witnessing the slow unfolding of the world around me like a love letter.

Love's Seeking and Finding

The poems in this section are inspired by all the ways we go looking for love or make ourselves available to it. Sometimes we then find it in ways we were not expecting. These are poems about desire and how the world around us can kindle that longing for something bigger. It can remind us that life is not just ruled by sorrow, but there is another kind of intelligence at work. Some of these poems are about listening to your encounters with all of your senses awakened to discover love beating there.

Love can feel slippery at times, sometimes a shy visitor, sometimes an undertow. We have moments when we know the depth of love at work in the world, and then we awaken and it has slipped through our fingers and all we can do is open our tender hearts again. It is only when we are willing to descend into the fullness of our vulnerability that the full strength of love is revealed.

Several of these poems are inspired by the mysteries of migration and how we as humans also feel a call or draw to other landscapes at times. Love pulls us toward a great unknown. Love bestows courage to let our wings pulse in a holy direction.

Bodies are also significant here—the touch of the human or an encounter with fur, fin, or feather. Sometimes we fall in love with the body of a mountain or a particular tree. Love is not a disembodied, ephemeral idea. It comes enfleshed. We know love by the aches, the pleasures, the shuddering heart, the exquisite deepening of our breath. Often our bodies feel the longing before the mind knows what it desires.

Dreams too can be a doorway to a deeper understanding of love's mysteries. Dreams often call us toward loving the difficult parts of ourselves and others. Sometimes our dreams reveal the seeking and finding of our hearts.

Six Portraits of Love

1.
Her small black dog
nuzzles, settles in,
rain caresses the windows.

2.
Massaging her mother's feet
under glare of hospital lights,
the crush of goodbyes.

3.
Their fingers laced together,
lines on skin a map
of all the roads they have traveled.

4.
He followed her across the ocean,
her heart a rose quartz
under eastern light.

5.

She awakens early to greet the sun,
an act of devotion,
pen stroking the page.

6.

She wanders among wet stones
and ruins, can hear ancient songs,
can feel the prayers of thousands.

If you were to write six portraits of love what would they be?
What are the moments of your life that witness to love's
meaning? What or who is the Muse to your inner longings?

I open to love in all of its forms, in beginnings and endings,
in quiet moments of presence, in the clamor of the world.

Longing

Consider
the swifts who
sleep on the wing,
the arrow of geese directed
to a faraway destination, the cuckoo
arriving each May in Ireland from Africa,
how the swallows pour from branches into air
like ink spilling across a blue page, sensing the invisible
current that will carry them to a place they know in the beating
of blood and wings and the promise of arrival.

We awaken to this longing too, sometimes
in the middle of the night. A steadiness
in our chests luring us like a lover
toward an unknowable goal,
asking us to follow
our desire

to take flight and defy gravity's pull.

*What longings awaken you from your slumbers,
whispering its desire to "come, follow me"? Can you leave
the certainty of now for the uncertainty of "what if"?
Where might your desire take you?*

*I watch migrations of birds and butterflies and I open to
that pull within my own heart.*

Corcomroe Abbey

If you pause
you can hear the whispered longings and wailings
carried across this threshold, the desperate cries
for healing, the shouts of praise, the stones are keepers
of these prayers, and to stand there is to feel
your heart both leap and break all at once.

The roof is gone which means this place
is no longer shielded from the elements but holds
its mouth up to catch raindrops on the tongue,
sunlight pours down and fills the space with gold.
The cawing of rooks nesting echoes off the walls,
nettles grow in corners, dandelions in cracks,
and you see this place is not a ruin, is not empty,
and you offer up a prayer, not certain who is listening,
but knowing this prayer does not live alone, but finds a place
nestled among birds and spirits and growing things.

Have you ever stood in a "ruin" but felt the presence of pilgrims and prayers in the stones? What is the prayer you want to whisper in that place?

I offer my prayers and know they are held by angels and ancestors, saints and wild things.

Migration

We drove north from Seattle for two hours
to see them, geese traveling from one faraway
place to another. Evening approaches early
in January, we turn down a side road
and follow the long field still wet
from afternoon rain. The sky is clearing
and clouds gather into piles of wool,
freshly shorn, tinted pink then lavender.

We see the gathering of hundreds –
a blur of down and beaks and webbed feet.
One single goose pushes up from soft
earth and lifts into the air, wings wide,

> then another
>
> > and another
> >
> > > and another.

We have stopped now along with a dozen
who have also come here to pray,
to let ourselves be lifted into the darkening sky,
our mouths have all dropped open,
a silent Alleluia erupting
as we imagine the trust in invisible pathways
and currents which carry them onward
as soon as they yield their bodies to the wind.

What have been the moments in nature that have suddenly lifted your heart higher than you thought possible? What might happen if you surrendered all your beliefs and certainties, and instead let yourself be lifted and carried along by nothing more than your trust that there is more than what you feel beneath your feet, that there is wonder and joy when you yield your Self to the freedom of Divine Unknowing?

I open my heart to the wisdom of winged ones –
geese and swans, monarchs and painted ladies –
and let my spirit be lifted on feather and current.

Beloved

Your body a cluster of grapes
sweet, filled with promise of wine

your lips pour moonlight
across open fields

your hands are maps
to secret universes

your eyes an invitation
to quiet forests

your back, stone face
a cliff rising

your teeth a row of white houses
saying welcome.

I love all of you: thigh tongue torso
hold nothing back from me beloved

your love a river where salmon
swim strong determined.

For now hold me with your eager arms
as we count the hours

each a globe of light
calling each one gift.

Has there been someone in your life who saw the beauty and wholeness of all of you?

I open my body to love, knowing it arrives by touch, taste, fragrance, music, vision, and intuition.

Everything Rises

Blue light of stars,
red richness of blood,
yellow warmth of sun,
green shoots of spring.

Hyssop, yarrow, woodruff,
each word a world,
an orbit around the sun —
wedge of lemon
explosion on the tongue,
smell of fresh melon,
give thanks for the first
bite of a summer cherry,
juice gushing over
parched lips.

No longer needing to seek,
you have been found by love.

*What are the experiences of summer that lift you from
your daily burdens? What drips like sweet nectar on your
tongue, calling out with every mouthful, that you have
arrived, what you have been seeking, you have found?*

*I let go of my striving, grasping, and seeking,
and allow myself to be found.*

You Did Not Come Here

You did not come here
to find yourself,
develop a master plan.

The gods are not awaiting
your self-realization
or enlightenment.

All that is asked of you
is to listen to the thumping
of your uncertain heart

to follow as it leads
you down through
ground dug up by doubt.

You must lay aside your idols
of control, doing, grasping,
breathe until everything softens,

until your fists unfold
until you feel your earthiness,
find soil where you can bloom.

How does your body feel when you let go of your self-improvement projects? How does your spirit feel when you release the need to make something happen? Can you see you are enough, that you have already found yourself, you were just too busy trying to be someone else to notice who you really are?

I soften my fists and simply allow life to bloom before and within me.

Suspended

The water asks only one thing
of her: to yield anything
that keeps her from love, until
she is no longer holding on,
not to the walls she carefully
built, not the wounds that tremble,
not even her own name,

until she can hear the lake calling
and she sees in the surface a mirror,
revealing herself to herself.
Instead of turning away
she draws closer, plunges
into sapphire depths,
realizes she is the water,

she is the sun's glow, she is
love's embrace enfolding
her, there was never a barrier,
just the world waiting for her
to say yes.

Have you ever gone swimming in a lake or ocean and felt the water lifting you up? What might happen if you could surrender your doubts and fears, all those obstacles which seem to arise like barriers between you and your heart's yearning?

I let go of anything that keeps me from love: barriers, resentments, misunderstandings.

You Know Now

Haws push through
tips of thorny branches, turn from green
to red, scent of meadowsweet

rises on wings of gladness
while pink blackberry blossoms
emerge with a song they've been waiting

for months to sing. You know now
that love erupts into the world as color
and melody, that you have not

been abandoned, but awakened
to a symphony of hues,
to make a home in the space

between notes, a doorway
to this quiet communion.

What are the colors of spring that gladden your heart?
Imagine living in a world where love is incarnated within
everything you see, hear, feel, touch, taste.

I listen for love's hues and music and let this spectrum
awaken my heart.

Secrets and Silence

Generosity of rain fills the forest
with patters and hums
(this rhythm so unlike clocks
ticking or calendar spaces),
branches droop low,
drops roll off as they sing
a song of surrender,
brown bed of leaves, soaked
and heavy.

There is a secret heard only
in silence, tree roots whisper
it through soil and stillness,
send it on feathers aloft as birds
lift from branches into air
scribing the sky with new promise.

Silence pours from the early sky,
wet and silver, trees tremble
in the wind, their humming
chorus calls me
to pause,
to still,
until I hear
the hush within,
seal my speech away
beneath the flat stones.

What is the song silence sings to you when you quiet your chatter? Can you feel your soul tremble in response to what it has heard?

I join the stillness of stars and stones, of ferns and forests. I let silence embrace me and infuse me until we are one.

Night Comes

Lavender first lures the eye
skyward, blue pushed out
to edges, making way
for pink wings spread wide,
then the violet urgency rises,
ripples, and recedes, opening
its charcoal mouth, swallows
the day's harsh gleam.
I sit and wait without words
and reach toward the slow glint
of stars emerging, my hands
look so small, they want
to scoop up the growing darkness
like a handful of secrets or whispers.

Do you ever make time to simply wait in stillness and silence for night to paint its way across the sky, colors changing hue until the stars emerge from blackness? What secrets does the arrival of nighttime whisper to you?

I trust in the wisdom of darkness and let it be a companion to me.

A Love Like This

There was the moment
you looked at me – not just with kindness
of friendship, but with something
more vibrant and lingering.
The moss green of your eyes fell into the moss
green of mine, and all the walls I had
carefully constructed began to tumble
– the way an old building crumples and falls
in on itself. I knew it was in your seeing
me and my seeing you there bloomed
a space, the way a morning glory opens
its petals under the persistent
gaze of the sun.

In the years that followed, the rubble
left inside me was carried away
like a glacier sweeping the land clear.
I fell more in love with you
each day, with life, even when it ached
to do so. We leaned into one another
as each one of our parents died,
followed one another from city
to city as new dreams erupted
in the darkness, knew

how blessed we were in an ocean
of loneliness. I made you promise
I could die first, so I wouldn't be left alone,
but when I did almost die I fought back
like a lion, like a dog with a bone,
to the presence of you, it was like pulling
a bucket up from a long dark well
and drinking the cold, clear water.

*Do you remember the moment of first falling in love with
someone or something? What are the colors, shapes, sounds,
and textures you associate with this experience?*

I drink freely from the well of love's refreshment.

The Wedding Dance

from a painting by Pieter Bruegel

You could lose yourself in music
the pulse and the twirl,
as wine pours like a river –
forms a moat round your heart.

You could find yourself
among sweat and swaying,
know your purpose not only
in toil, but also delight.

Slow kisses and fast dances,
away from church's dour gaze,
branches dance too
in the vigorous breezes.

Gladness spreads through limbs
like an upturned bottle of ink,
the bride's hair tumbles free,
the couple kneels in soft grass.

Have you ever lost yourself in the whirl of joy-filled freedom, embraced by the happiness of love's desire? What have been the moments when dance set something free inside of you?

I lose myself in music, setting aside the tasks of the day, to sway and dance.

The Kiss

from a painting by Gustav Klimt

Her arms encircle him —
a halo of intensity.

Wrapped together in a cloak
they are twin stars

in a faraway galaxy pulsing
with impossible light.

his breath on her cheek like sunlight
after many winter days.

Their lips are plums,
filled with juice.

She is on her knees,
an ancient prayer,

with each moan the meadow
beneath them erupts in a riot

of amethyst and citrine petals.
She closes her eyes to breathe in

until she has become flower,
a golden sky wraps itself around her.

Have you ever lost yourself in the embrace of another?
Have your prayers ever felt like moans emerging from the
depths of your interior life?

Imagine lying down on a sunlit field,
letting all of creation hold you.

Goldfish

We traveled more than 5000 miles
to a new life and there stood a water barrel
waiting outside the courtyard door,
two goldfish circling, one yellow,
one white and gold, darting in and out
of swaying greenery, dancing among
the bubbles.

We had arrived to Vienna on Gustav Klimt's
150th birthday, the city was celebrating,
so we named these new companions Gustav
and Klimt, looking like they had emerged
from the gold fields of The Kiss.

The wooden barrel stood waist high,
present each time we crossed the threshold
for our leavings and arrivings.
I'd touch a finger to the surface
to say hello or goodbye, Gustav dashed away,
Klimt was curious, bolder, bumping
against me, making himself known.

In summer, the sun shimmered across
the water's surface, in autumn jeweled
leaves landed like tiny boats.
Winter turned the surface solid
and they descended below the frozen
floating circle. We left before spring
so they are still there in my mind
resting and dreaming, like sunken treasure.

*Do you practice any rituals whenever you are about to cross a
threshold between here and there? How might such a practice
transform your understanding of all your "leavings and
arrivings," the letting go of what has been, and the welcoming
of what gifts the presence brings?*

I trust in the wisdom of the seasons, each revealing its own gift.

A Story in Five Tattoos

I

In the days after my mother died
butterflies arrived like tiny angels
so I had one penned on my ankle,
the artist wiped away the bleeding,
the pain nothing like my heart's rending.

II

My grandmother died six months
after I was born, left me with a photo
of her dancing now imprinted on my leg,
one arm a halo above her head,
the other lifting her dress, on quiet nights
her longing makes my feet tremble.

III

I moved across the Atlantic
and suddenly pears were everywhere —
in stories told, my dreams, on store shelves
— their round sweet bodies now stenciled
on my arm, telling me there is always
more than enough.

IV

Twenty-five years of marriage,
we joked finally we were ready
for real commitment, your initial "J"
on my arm, illuminated with those
unending Celtic knots, my skin
the parchment.

V

The next one will be a cuckoo bird
like the one that called for an hour
from my father's grave one May afternoon,
trickster in feathers, the goddess Laima
of fate travels with one,
what destiny will she reveal to me?

Do you have any symbolic tattoos? If not, what might be an image that would feel significant enough to mark yourself with?

I pay attention to the signs around me ushering me into the next season of my life.

Map is Not Territory

I want to trace my finger along the edges of you,
come to know every divot by heart,
in the same way you run a finger
along a river on an old map.

I can't hear the secrets whispered
beyond its shores by reading the atlas
I only know these things by sitting at the edge,
listening to the music water makes as it traverses stone.

After so many years so much of you is still
unknowable. I delight in each new revelation,
hope to never stop being an explorer,
to never complete this journey of discovery.

*What are the layers of mystery you keep discovering in a lover
or soul friend? When have you felt yourself to be an explorer of
landscapes, inner and outer, previously unknown to you?*

*I commit to always being a pilgrim, never having fully arrived
or fully understood.*

She Is All Feather

Some days she lands in the shape of a robin
her song an invocation
to the bright fields of sky.

Some days she swoops past me as a heron,
flash of gray and I feel my life enlarge
every part of me stretching open,

Some days she is the solitary crow,
wings thumping against cold wind,
my bones shudder.

Today she is a swan in the silence
of my aloneness. She calls forth something
I've only known when death came close,
carving out an echoing cave,
filled it with music.

What are the birds that call to you in a special way?
What is the bird you meet calling forth from you?

I open to wisdom in feathered forms, teaching me
grace in living.

Dreams

To
willingly
descend the long
dark staircase is an
act of trust that something
worthwhile waits for you there
in the cellar with its cobwebbed boxes
piled high with discarded things, the scent
of a mouse long dead and naphthalene balls.

Some days you clamber around, eyes not yet adjusted
to this night territory, so everything you bump startles
you. But some days your pupils widen and you wander
in amazement, seeing just how much light is contained
in darkness, like stones shimmering in moonlight,
and rather than return with a pile of them,

you choose one to carry back up the stairs,
back into the comfort of your home,
where this tiny gift splits open
the foundation. You look out
where the window once
was, and instead of
the brick wall of
the house next
door, you
realize
you can now see to the horizon.

What is your relationship to your nighttime and daytime dreaming? What "tiny gift" have you discovered in your dream world, carrying it back up from your unconscious mind into your waking mind? What message did this dream image hold for you?

I allow my dreams to break down walls I've created so I can see the sky more clearly.

The Doorway

You arrived in a dream and even though
I'd spent years trying to sail across
the canyon between us, here you were,
reaching toward me, gray hair still thick
and wild, rising from your widow's peak,
the green eyes I inherited
searching my face. We both turned
toward the western sky where October's
amber light gleamed, pouring over us
like honey, and I said *It's okay Daddy,*
you can walk into the light now,
my breath scraping my throat,
hardly believing
this moment had finally come
eighteen years after your hasty
leaving, after I had walked again
and again in all the places
you once loved in search of
a secret doorway. You arrived now
as if to acknowledge all my effort,
as if to ask me to send you forth
into that glorious, irresistible light
and I felt something more like love
for you than I could ever remember.

Who are the people in your family or life who have been challenging to love? What landscapes serve as portals to your inner soul-scape? Have you discovered the "secret doorway" offering solace for your burning questions and life quests?

I open my heart to the grace of healing and all the ways it might arrive.

Dog Dreams

In the middle of the forest there's an unexpected clearing
that can only be found by those who have gotten lost.
—Tomas Tranströmer

You press your body against me, black fur
breathing softly, toes twitching,
muffled growls from closed lips,
and I follow you down the staircase
of dreams where we stand together
in a gathering of trees. *I wanted to bring you here*
you bark and I understand every word.
Your tail makes circles of joy as you dart
off into the woods following your hunter's nose.
I lose sight of your dark coat in a sea of ferns
and moss. *Wait*, I cry, but I can't keep up.
Your name becomes a prayer I call
again and again.

I turn off the path into green thickness,
snapping through branches as I pass,
I run so far and so long until nothing
looks familiar, and I pause to rest scanning
the unfamiliar trees. You appear
in a clearing ahead with brown eyes bright,
tail still wagging with vigor, pink tongue

waving like a flag, delighting in this game
of following where our noses lead us,
letting scents of underearth spur us
onward, even if it means getting lost,
where all the best things are found.

Who are the animal companions who have taught you about
life and love? When was the last time you willingly followed the
path of your intuition, letting go of the map, at ease with the
possibility of getting lost? What did you find?

I let go of maps and allow myself to get lost.

Where has the wild woman gone?

I have seen her bathing
in the lake, long hair drying
in the breeze. She sits
on a stone at the water's edge
for hours and does nothing.
Her teeth have bits of dandelion
leaf stuck between them. She still
composes those poems you are
so fond of, but she sings them
into the air, finds words tracked
across sky in cloud and star. Each tree,
under her gaze, becomes its own
poem. She waits for you there,
knowing there is nothing but time.

She is the one you left behind when you
traded your bark for papers, your
stones for pens, and the sun's
pilgrimage across the horizon
for your calendar with its tidy
color-coded boxes.

When you wake from a dream
one morning and smell

oak leaves dissolving into
the forest floor, you know this
is a love letter from her to you.

No matter your gender, what does the wild woman
in you look life? Smell like? Feel like?
What signs in your life indicate their presence?

I look and listen for love letters my wild self has left for me in
the scent of moss or fierceness of storm.

Dreaming of Ascent

The music starts so softly I strain to hear it.
My hips move in slow circles, the piano
intensifies and my feet slide across
the waxed-wood floor gaining momentum.
The cello enters and my body turns round
and round on an unknown axis. I realize
my feet are no longer touching down,
I can feel the air swirling beneath my toes.
The drumbeat enters and I want to stomp, but
instead of hitting ground, each footfall propels
me higher until the roof opens like a box lid
of a surprise gift, flutes now contribute
their melody, lifting me with each breath
into sky where I am surrounded by starlings
swerving and swooping, the current
continues to raise me upward and I am
breathing in clouds and blue, the music
intensifies but it now comes from the sun.
I can hear the harmony of the spheres and I am
flickering starlight. Earth recedes from view
until it is a pinpoint of light in a sea of sparks.
I am a dancer in an ocean of song.

What magical places have your dreams transported you to? Have you ever felt yourself lifted beyond the boundaries of your physical being so that for a moment you could hardly distinguish yourself from everything that enveloped?

I allow music to propel me among galaxies, each note, the stars swirling, each silence, the darkness expanding.

The Gift

She pulls at the purple ribbon
    and lets it slide off the star-stamped
        paper, tears at it eagerly
            like a child on Christmas morning.
        Inside is a box covered in tiny mirrors.
    Sunlight reflects all around the room
creates fireflies dancing on walls.
    She catches glimpses of her green eyes
        and the soft lines circling them
            like tributaries on a map.
        She tilts it and sees her curtain
    of brown hair falling across her face,
her smile gets wider with each turn
    of the box in her hands. It keeps
        dazzling and she is dancing now,
            all her haloed faces refracted,
                revolving around an axis of joy.

Have you ever received a gift that helped you to see yourself in
a new way or transported you to a time outside time?
What happens within when you recall such an infinity of joy,
encapsulated in just a few brief moments?
Do you still believe in joy and the possibility of happiness?

I keep my hands open, ready to receive the gift meant for me.

Where I Want to Live

Forgive yourself if after the year
that's passed you need to sleep
for a dozen circles of the sun
and hold the world back.

When you finally emerge again,
a mole peering out from its den,
you can breathe deeply.
Open your hands and sit

and wait for a sunlit evening
in autumn, or splash of a cold river,
or the hour before sunrise
watching light pour back into the cup

of the world, for love to return first
as a shy visitor, then take up
residence in your dreams,
claiming this house as her own.

Where do you want to live? What is the season or time of day that most calls to you? What happens when you sit quietly in the lap of nature, watching and waiting without expectancy or preordained ideas, just glad to be present to the hours of the earth? What arrives to "take up residence" in your inner world?

I allow myself the fulness of rest and then move slowly through the magic of the world.

The Love of
the Ancestors

The ancestors first called to me when my mother died. I was completely bereft, and reaching out to my father, my mother, my grandparents, and the generations before them was at times excruciatingly hard, at other times magnificent. It always led ultimately to greater healing.

The poems in this section reflect many of the conversations, wonderings, and journeys I have made to connect with my forebears of blood and bone. I write my way back into the stories that have been forgotten, the inheritance that has gone unclaimed.

Whether we know where we came from or not, I believe our ancestors call to us through our DNA. They beg us to help heal their wounds. They gift us with their shimmering blessings. Their longings echo in our dreams, our own secret desires. We may wonder why the scent of lilac makes us want to weep or why the way the forest meets the sea feels like a place of such ripe possibility for us.

As the Chicksaw poet and author Linda Hogan writes in her book *Dwellings: A Living History of the Natural World*: "You are the result of the love of thousands." No matter how dysfunctional your family may have been, you only have to go back a few generations to reach thousands of ancestors. Imagine the love that drew so many of them together to bring you into being.

What I discovered was that in the process of trying to heal my father's wounds, I was set free. While speaking aloud the stories of my grandmothers, I discovered a deeper sense of purpose. In researching the names on different lines I kept finding myself in awe and in love with these people who had struggled with their humanity before me. They also longed for love and sometimes showed up for it fully and sometimes not.

Field Notes on Being an Orphan

(after Mary Jean Chan)

And yes my father died suddenly and I felt such great
relief and yes my mother died almost as suddenly and the
grief debilitated me for years and yes I was already 33 when I
officially became an orphan so you might think I'm overstating
my case and yes I know that Oscar Wilde famously wrote to
lose one parent is a tragedy, but to lose both is careless and
yes I felt compelled to piece together my family tree, to come
to know my ancestors even though I have no children to pass
it onto and yes it feels like I must do this before I die and if
I stop doing it I will die and yes I have no siblings to share
this specific grief and find myself drawn to friends who are
motherless and fatherless, like we're a secret communion, and
yes I find myself coming alive when I cook my mother's red
cabbage recipe and when I play classical music and a Strauss
waltz comes on I must take my husband's hand and awkwardly
sweep him across the floor and yes I remember my tiny bare
feet standing on my father's shoes as he counted out 1, 2, 3
and yes I have traveled across Europe to walk the lands of my
grandmothers and grandfathers, to breathe that air, to let it fill
me, to feel myself not so alone, and yes I did one day forgive
my father, it came in a flash, without any effort at all, although

I had worked hard at it for years, and yes suddenly I knew the freedom I had longed for, felt what I imagine the wind feels like as the geese open their wings, fall into formation, and ride the current toward the horizon.

Have you lost one or both parents? What are the memories you treasure? What has been your experience of forgiveness? Was it difficult, or did it feel impossible? If impossible, can you imagine the sense of freedom which might set you loose from the chains that have bound you to this thing that happened in the past? Might it be possible for you too to "ride the current toward the horizon" and free yourself in the very moment when you forgive the past?

I surrender to the freedom that awaits me and let it carry me higher.

Autobiography

I am the soft manicured hands of my mother
bruised from tubes sustaining her life.

I am the furrowed brow of my father,
beneath his widow's peak, the longing for drink.

I am my grandmother's Art Deco diamond ring
that she wore to dozens of balls

I am my grandfather's arms rowing
the oars of the canoe far from shore.

I am the bones of my ancestors,
sinew, tendon, muscle, blood,
skulls painted with spring flowers.

Do you experience the presence of your ancestors who are living still in your bones and body? What emerges for you when you consider that you are just one single point in a long line of ancestral birthings and dyings?
Reflecting upon this, who are you now?
If you wrote your own autobiography poem,
what would you include?

I honor those who walked before me, struggling and loving as best they could.

First Kiss

That they would all be joined
together in this moment,
his ancestors and mine cheering us
on as our lips met for the first time,
how his kiss taught me what words
could never, that grief does not last forever,
that the loving gaze of another is enough
to wake us up to the truth about ourselves,
and even now after thousands more kisses,
after learning that pleasure is so sweet,
never to be resisted, how the elders
know this and from behind the veil
love me for saying yes.

Do you remember your first kiss? Is there someone in your life the ancestors would celebrate you connecting with? How does it feel to imagine them willing you on to a life of joy? What will you do next, knowing that those from whom you emerge are kissing you in a stream of illuminated blessings, wishing only that you might live a life of freedom and happiness?

I say yes to the sweetness that the pleasure of connection offers me.

I Come from People

(after Kim Moore)

I come from people who dragged nets of fish
from the Atlantic, could smell it on their hands
and clothes long into the night.

I come from people who stood at the shore
of the Baltic Sea, watching Solstice bonfires
in the waters, rippling outward.

I come from men wearing soldier's uniforms,
torn, blood-stained, medals rusting in the dresser.
I come from rabbis and ministers,
grocers and lawyers, businessmen
opening another new store.

I come from women who loved to teach and dance,
but once married were forbidden such
suspicious joys anymore, who danced in secret
before children awakened, hiding
calloused feet in slippers,
who told stories of the one-room schoolhouse
and kept a piece of chalk in the drawer to smell.

Where did your people come from? How did they labor? Can you open your inner eye to sense their secret dances, the hidden mementos of their dreams and longings? In what way might you honor the lives they yearned to live?

I offer gratitude for all the grace my ancestors brought into the world and grief for all the wounding they caused.

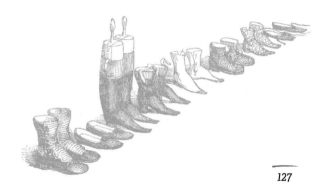

Sorrow

When my mother died
it was the forest
that held me close:

the soft floor,
the leaf-tiled sky,
the air, fresh

like a cold spring
I wanted to gulp
on a summer day.

There was room for me
and all my sorrow
among fern, moss,

and maple leaves
twirling toward earth.
I was the letting go

and the landing,
the stripping away
and the skeleton

of branches remaining,
I was the dark earth holding
seeds not yet ready to open.

What has been your experience of grief and loss? Did you make room for all your sorrowing to express itself in any way it felt called? Are you still holding grief "not yet ready" to release and let go? How will you honor this loss that still lives within?

I go among trees and let them hold me as I weep.

Awakening

I wake from a dream,
my ancestors dance
in field and forest
and my feet tremble,
my bones fill with music.

I wake from a dream,
my ancestors weep
by graves and piles of ash,
my eyes spill and splash,
my blood is brine.

Every moment of laughter
glimmers across time,
an echo of joy,
each cry and wail
a thread of sorrow
stitching together the garment
of generations, a cloak
under which joy and sorrow kiss,
emptying me out
to be filled
with delight.

Have your ancestors ever appeared in a dream?

*I make space for laughter and weeping in equal measure.
I imagine my ancestral line as a thread woven through
time, stitched into a garment of memories made of
happiness and sadness.*

Mothers

My mother and his mother
died eight years and twenty days apart.
Both gave a week or so notice
of their impending departure
so we had time to sit vigil
with their bodies already growing slack.
How brittle and shrunken they had become,
once vessels for so much love.

Maybe they both dreamed of their own mother's touch,
the first drops of milk into searching mouths
or that first inhale, maybe all the moments
when love filled them came rushing back
before that final exhale, where something
slipped free from each and took something
of us with them.

Have you ever sat vigil with someone?

What was your relationship to those who mothered you?

I honor death as part of life's sweet circle.

As She Lay Dying

Her body covered with plastic tubes,
transport for breath, blood, dialysis,
urine, a rush hour traffic of beeps
and hums, her skin a diaphanous scarf
draped over veins and bones.

One wall is half window
with a curtain of trees below.
Staring through glass
I am suddenly bird. I push off
from the sill and soar above
the manicured lawn, above the road
that leads here, and I ride the current
over undulations of land to the mountains,
row after row of stone breasts and hips
breathing under white blankets,
streams carry snowmelt,
like the hospital tubes,
down to the wide lake below.
I fly just above its surface,
see my coal-colored body reflected.
I drop from the sky and plunge
through the water's mirror

and I am by her side again
although soaked through now, trembling,
my back aches where wings once were.
Fly, I whisper to her, *fly*.

What words of benediction might you cry out to your
loved ones as they depart this realm to enter another
both near and far from where we now stand?

I let my imagination carry me across the wide
landscape so I return feeling enlarged.

Standing at My Mother's Grave

She is a constellation,
at first only the thick
blackness is visible,

a heavy wool blanket I want
to throw off myself.
if only I could move

but slowly my eyes adjust
and all those points of light
emerge and I see patterns

and I am like a pioneer
making discoveries in the dark:
a bear, an archer, a lover,

and I remember how stars
explode and vanish
a million miles away

while their light travels
and lingers for lifetimes.

Have you stood at the grave of a loved one? In what way does the memory of a lost loved one still linger in your life? What images recall your beloved to your heart and mind?

I lie down under a night sky to see the faces of my ancestors in the gathering of stars.

I Dream of My Mother

We drive along the California coast highway
in a shiny red convertible with room
for your wheelchair in back.
You tell me to drive because you want
to take in the view. You hold up a pink pinwheel
you've brought and giggle as it twirls round
in summer wind. You point at things —
a pelican, a hot air balloon, a kite
— and I remind you I'm driving so my eyes
stay fixed on the road. I catch a glimpse
of you from the corner of my eye,
your big sunglasses, silk scarf fluttering,
pomegranate lips revealing coffee-stained
teeth. You say something about being
like Thelma and Louise and I remind you
it doesn't end well for them. I look
in the rearview mirror. My eyes look tired
and I can see the sun setting. The orange
globe of light slowly disappears from view.

If you had a waking dream about a loved one who died where would you want to travel together? Do your lost loved ones ever visit you in your dreams? What messages do these images hold forth for you, like gifts from another world?

I make space to remember those I love in full color.

On the Edge

The album pages stick together,
old glue turning the color of mustard,
images fading like wisps of smoke.
I come to the page that always
made my parents laugh out loud

– there I am, Kodak-preserved, age 2,
face purple, mouth contorted, eyes red,
body perched on my crib's edge.
Somehow I have lifted myself up one side
and realized I can't go over
without falling to the faraway floor.
Going back behind the bars
of my confinement
doesn't seem possible anymore –

every time they laugh my body hardens
like a tire iron as I realize I cried out,
suspended, and my parents grabbed
their camera first before rescuing me.

I am still there, as we all are,
perched between cage
and terrifying freedom,
crying out for love and saving,
hoping only for an arm, a hand.

Can you recall times when you felt yourself hovering dangerously on the precipice between certainty behind and intimidating freedom in front of you? Might this be a metaphor for stepping off the perimeters of certitude and instead letting yourself fall into the unknown with unwavering trust that it will catch you, rescuing you from yourself?

I give myself the safety and support I need.
I extend that love back to my child self.

The Letter

I opened the envelope slowly
dreading the words inside.
I knew what you might say –
and you didn't disappoint
– but instead of emptiness
as you receded from me, I felt filled
with something like love.
My dreams consoled me with banquets
piled with fruits to fill my hunger,
they led me down pathways
into the sunlit forest, a communion
with light. I knew these as truth
the way a dream turns
your understanding inside out,
can turn the heartbreak of loneliness
into kindness.
I realize you no longer define
the limits of my world.
It's bursting at the seams.

Did a loved one ever break your heart? What consoled you in your journey of grief and healing?

I let my loneliness be transformed by compassion into kindness. I see the loneliness in others and extend my hand.

Riga

1944, the year you fled as Russians stampeded,
you and your sister grasping the soft hand
of your mother on the long train ride through
the night. Your father followed much later,
while your aunt was sent on to Siberia.

And from there a door slammed shut inside
and you kept the stories secret even though
the old photo albums show photos of you
as a boy playing by the Baltic Sea,
a curtain of trees behind you.

I know there was ice cream and sand pails,
swimming and giggles. But the winters were
dark and cold, and soon a fire began to burn
the cathedral tower, a wild flame scattering
the past. Once you left, this place became
a distant echo, a cavern you filled with
Johnny Walker Red and Bloody Marys.

I traveled there years after you left
this bright world. It felt like a door sealed shut
was pried open, rusty hinges crying out,
a path into a garden choked by weeds
and a single wild rose emerging,
the one whose scent makes me think of you,
the one I had to write about, to speak aloud.

What are the traumas your ancestors endured that sealed shut doors inside them? What lies hidden, waiting to be excavated and opened out into the luminous light of truth?
Is there any image arising which reflects your understanding of the past, the lives of those before you?

I will tell the stories that have been hidden away.

Ludwig

My father always traced the family tree
to you, showing our relation to the Wittgensteins.
When I majored in philosophy in college
he thought it was perfect, though I didn't study you
at the time, turned off by logic.

At midlife I moved to Vienna,
then because of bureaucracy's coldness
moved on to the west of Ireland
to find solace by the Atlantic
and the sea's wild foam, to get my bearings,
not giving you another thought
until one day I learned that you
were drawn here too, had lived among
those granite mountains just an hour's drive
from me at the mouth of Killary fjord.

You called Connemara "the last pool
of darkness," the only place you could
think clearly. Suddenly I knew
how I had also ended up here,
a lover of wild silence,
of winter's dark stillness, a compass
in my blood, and now I can't stop
thinking of you.

I've spent days in the cottage next door
to where you lived until I could hear
the mountain outside my window
whisper secrets about you.
I traveled to Prague to visit the graves
of rabbis, ancestors we share.
I journeyed to Norway to stand
by the cottage you built across the lake
sitting in shadows and quiet
and visited the house in Vienna you designed,
so spare it felt like walking into your mind

In private moments I started calling
you *cousin Ludwig*. I want to know
how you endured all those times
you wanted to leave this life,
the people you loved. I want to know
as if my life depended on it,
like someone lost might search
for a map or a star.

Is there something in your life that you badly need to know?
Where are the stars and maps that guide the wandering and
the lost which might help you find what you are looking for?
Is there a special soul landscape where the answer might lie
hidden, waiting for you to find it?

I look to my ancestors for guidance on my path.

Snow Globe

It was snowing in July.
1900 meters up the slate slope
boots tightly laced,
my yellow raincoat with strawberries —
a brightness against the dark sky.
You in your green Loden coat
long wool socks pulled over your calves
walking stick in hand.
The weather was not an impediment;
we had come here to hike
and snow in July meant
the world was slightly upside down.
My child legs running to keep up,
Your legs moved in quick strides
as though you longed to be elsewhere.
While passing Alpine cows
I'd touch their broad soft noses.
You holding my hand now,
humming a waltz to make the journey easier,
the distance between us suddenly smaller.
It was snowing in July and
the world was upside down.
How much longer? I'd always ask.
You'd point to the next bend.

Finally the arrival at the hut for soup.
Warmth spreading through me,
we'd sit facing each other
there on the mountaintop.
You were mine
in that snow globe upside down.

In that snow globe upside down
you were mine
there on the mountaintop.
We'd sit facing each other
warmth spreading through me.
Finally the arrival at the hut for soup.
You'd point to the next bend.
How much longer? I'd always ask.
The world was upside down
it was snowing in July and
the distance between us suddenly smaller –
humming a waltz made the journey easier.
You holding my hand now.
I'd touch those broad soft noses
while passing Alpine cows.
As though you longed to be elsewhere
your legs moved in quick strides,
my child legs running to keep up.
The world was slightly upside down

and snow in July meant
we had come here to hike.
Weather was not an impediment.
Walking stick in hand
long wool socks pulled over your calves
you in your green Loden coat
a brightness against the dark sky.
My yellow raincoat with strawberries
boots tightly laced
1900 meters up on the slate slope.
It was snowing in July.

*Can you recall a time in your life when the boundaries between
you and another became more fluid and aery, allowing your
souls to open wide to the presence of the other as a mingling
of spiritual selves, all obstacles washed out in a river of pure,
unsullied love?*

*I make time to remember and cherish the moments
that I want to endure.*

My Grandmother Loved Lilacs

I bury my face into their soft hands,
gulp down their honeyed perfection
and anything seems possible

even summoning you here, corners
of your pinched mouth softening,
your restless hands, having knit me
dozens of cardigans, now still.

A song is playing only we can hear,
the one you loved to sway your hips to
when nobody was looking,
your fingers clutch the kite string
of purple scent ascending.

*What scents carry memories of loved ones lost? Can you open
yourself to the gifts of the sensuous earth, allowing it to evoke
portals which can transform quotidian time into eternal
time, where what was is present to you again like a prayer
supplicating visions of those who have crossed the threshold of
our time? Do you feel that "anything seems possible"?*

*I pause to inhale the fragrance of everything blooming
into this world.*

After My Grandmother Died

My mother opened her dresser drawer
and found it full of pills.
My grandmother had reason for despair:
growing up in the Great Depression,
with a schizophrenic sister,
and giving up the teaching
she loved to marry.

Now her always pinched face
and distant eyes made sense.
I became an archaeologist of my life,
unearthing all that had hardened
generations ago, even if it meant
putting them now on display,
no longer hidden and dusty.
I polished those bones until
they gleamed like a smile,
until I could carve them hollow
and play their song.

How might you become an "archaeologist" of your life?
In what ways might you begin to unveil the hurts of ancestors
who saved themselves in the only way they could?
Are you open to the possibility of healing ancient wounds
and, in the process, healing yourself too?

I dig up secrets like bones, removing grit and grime,
holding them to the light.

I want to be the kind of woman

(after Jenni Fagan)

I want to be the kind of woman
who milks goats each morning
and drinks straight from the bucket –
who isn't afraid to reach into the hive.

I want to be the kind of woman
who lies down in winter,
in the brown mulch of leaves
and sleeps until spring
who loves the generous folds of her body.

I want to be the kind of woman
who has found her sealskin,
who would cross oceans to make
her dead father love her once again.

I want to be the kind of woman
who can name hyssop, nettle, lady's mantle
and knows all their healing uses.

I want to be the kind of woman
who goes out under the night sky
to chant with owls and wolves,

who falls more in love each day
with her husband, her little dog, her life.

I want to be the kind of woman
who knows she is daughter of sunlight and mud
who knows that her grandmothers
are still singing her name.

What is the kind of person you want to be?
What images shimmer with meaning for you?
How might you embrace this vision as the manifestation
of your soul's deepest desire?

I hear the song of my ancestors each morning
singing me into a new day.

Grandmother

I was born before the two Great Wars
with a birthmark on my ankle
in the shape of a rose,
an ancient spell cast on me
that sparked my feet to dance,
so I spent years with toes pointed,
arms circling the air.

I was dancing in my mind
the day I skipped up those marble stairs
and ran into the man who'd whisk me
from Vienna to Riga
where I gave birth to a boy and girl
ten minutes apart.
I'd hand them over to nannies
while we danced for hours at parties,
around ice sculptures and trays of pâté.
He made it clear early on, dance would be kept
in a box and he held the key, only opening it
when suitable. My body slowly shriveled
as I kept the gestures to myself.

Our babies had babies and now
a hundred years later I am in a room
filled with loud music, I hate the sound but

my body is young again and I can't help but
respond, I could not stop if I wanted to,
decades of dance spilling into this
new moment like a fountain, feet calloused
again, a box opened, never to be shut again.

Is there something your ancestor loved that has become
a passion of your own? How are the expectations and
admonitions of others shrivelling your soul? What gestures
do you long to practice to sing your soul into being?
What's stopping you now?

I dance like a fountain gushing, grateful for the gift of this life.

The Love
of the Mystics

This section is devoted to the love that the mystics witness to in the world. Like the ancestors, the saints and mystics are those who have passed through the veil before us but continue to offer us guidance and wisdom. They continue to imagine love, send love, embody love through their teaching and presence.

When the world feels especially difficult to love, which can be most days, I can call upon mystics like Francis, Benedict, or Julian to reveal to me a new way of seeing. They look through eyes of sacred vision to discover love pulsing throughout creation. They know love as the foundation of all that exists. I can lean upon their spirits to help me find love around and within me once again.

They too are part of the "love of thousands" I mentioned at the start of the last section. They walked this earth with a desire to be transformed by love's call. They wanted to love those who were difficult to love. When we have an encounter with the divine and we feel inspired to love more, we can be assured the encounter was authentic. Our moments of sacred meeting always move us toward falling more and more in love with the world.

Let Me Sow Love

Where there is hatred, let me sow love.
—prayer attributed to St. Francis of Assisi

A wolf circles the town walls
with jaws ready to tear apart.
Francis opens the gate, extends
a steady hand, the wolf whimpers,
rolls onto his back, reveals his soft belly.
*

Forty days fasting on the mountaintop,
he wakes from a dream with hands, feet,
side bleeding, knows the agony of torture
and abandonment, his tears flow freely,
they bathe the red circles on his palms.
*

Her name was Clare, meaning light,
and her devotion unlocked something
inside him. Her hair chopped short
and her body struggled, but she saw the world
from her bed, knew it like a lover.
*

He called Death his sister, nursing lepers
he knew the body as delicate as the first
primrose in spring's fierce winds, knew
how the end could be a teacher,
a doorway to a new beginning.

He stands smiling in the town square,
has removed the weight
of silk and velvet garments,
some are shocked, while others long
to feel the hot sun prickle their skin.

*Where are the places of hatred in your life you could begin
to sow love? What earthy images reflect the fragility of your
warm, human body? What might it be like to live with this
knowledge of your portending death as if it were a call
to new life and new beginnings?*

I call on Brother Francis to teach me the ways of love.

St. Benedict Awakens

A shawl is being knit across the sky
pale pink and purple hues are cascading.
Darkness unravels, night's ash scattering.
Each bright morning when he first awakens
he rests there with eyes closed, breath slow, waiting,
for dreams to take root, for birdsong to start,
to feel sunlight travel across his face
spilling warmth in its honey golden wake.
For a moment hard memories dissolve
like salt in broth, like sunlight in a storm
and the world is no longer this or that
but fused together like colors in glass.
The first bell rings, calling him to prayer,
but Lauds has already begun here now.

What is your relationship to morning? When was the last time you rose just before the first gimmers of dawn began to awaken the world? How did everything appear in all its radiant translucence? What would it be like to invite the treasures of each dawning day into your spiritual practice?

I call on Brother Benedict to teach me how to begin the day in love, with love, and for love.

Julian of Norwich in Her Sick Bed

The stone walls stay cool on this late summer afternoon.
Bushels of golden apple light tumble through my small
    window,
casting a yellow square on the floor
which shifts slowly all day like a tired pilgrim.
The tabby cat places herself into this warm glow,
sighing each hour as she rises again to follow its journey.

A breeze rustles in and I gulp down autumn's early arrival
like being under a waterfall.
All day I watch the sun travel, the cat shift,
the snail who makes its way up my wall leaving a trail
like the tears that streak my face into a map of desire.

At night I dream I can fly, slip out the window into the dark
    liquid sky,
feel the night lift me onto her back like a wave cresting
and I am suddenly more than these frozen limbs,
I can taste the stars, flakes of sea salt sprinkled across
    black silk.

The moon opens her wide mouth as if to sing,
then swallows me, takes me inside her

until I know myself as one who waxes and wanes, who shines
    brightly
and sometimes disappears into darkness.

*What has been your experience of illness or forced
convalescence? Do you feel the rhythms of the moon reverberate
through your being so that you become one like her, wandering
through periods of waxing and waning, becoming and letting
go? Can you embrace these nocturnal rhythms as the natural
course of your earthly presence and being?*

*I call on Sister Julian to show me how to slow down and savor
the world so I might fall more deeply in love with it.*

Closing

Some Closing Thoughts on Love

This book of poems, questions, affirmations, and reflections is not meant to be a comprehensive look at the power of love in the world. It is written from the experience of one woman, living on the wild edges of Ireland, who tries as hard as she can to love well.

The title of this book, *Love Holds You*, is a statement of faith. It is not something that can be proven. The purpose of poetry is not to establish scientific propositions but to invite you into an experience. Poems are moments and ways of seeing the world. My hope is that through these various lenses you have found yourself a little more sure of the love that pulses through you, through those around you, through all of creation, and even through the ground beneath your feet. Some poems may have succeeded at that, others likely not. It is just an offering, an invitation into trust and then to see what you notice and experience from there.

Whatever I Find

hidden among the stones piled
by lake's edge – a beetle, a coin,
a candy wrapper – let it be a portent,
a cypher. Let me seek a new
direction among what is hidden,
lost, discarded, rather than always
grasping at some bright,
invisible future.

Have you ever found something on the ground that became an important symbol for your life? What soul landscapes do you willingly enter seeking harbingers of news from otherworldly realms, symbols and icons of a different way of inhabiting this life? Can you relinquish your illusory desires in favor of embracing the hidden gifts of now?

I stay alert to shimmering gifts that reveal some new direction.

ACKNOWLEDGMENTS

Every book is a collaborative effort. The words you see are inspired by a lifetime of conversations and encounters with others. This is probably even more true when it comes to poetry. Poems arise from the spaces between life moments, when we allow enough time to savor and digest and process what has happened. We can then offer it back to the world, not as a neat and tidy parcel with answers, but with a space to hold the mysteries and possibilities the world always offers to us.

I have been married to my husband, John, for 29 years the year this book is published. Together we have explored all the dimensions married love offers. Some days it has felt like work to keep on loving, but most days love has been a marvelous grace. I am extraordinarily grateful for the healing that being loved unconditionally has brought to my life. Each day I fall more in love.

I am also grateful to many dear friends who have helped me learn how to love as well as those in my life who are challenging to love, how they call the best out from me.

Special thanks goes to Edith O'Nuallain who assisted with crafting some of the reflection questions in this book. She is a dear friend and has a special gift of inviting others into the spaces between words and finding a deeper call there through a beautiful question.

Gratitude as well to Paraclete Press for being such enthusiastic supporters of my work and giving my poetry a publishing home. In this volume, in particular, they invited me to stretch a bit past a conventional poetry collection and create something even more engaging for my readers. It was a delightful dance to enter into.

Thank you to the Source of all Love, who is the sacred foundation and the holy direction, the ground and summit of my experience of love in the world and who creates all beings from this generous wellspring. Each morning I soak in prayers of gratitude for this primal awareness and how it carries me back into the world ready to love again. Each moment offers the possibility of devotion, each day brings a gift of something or someone to love into greater wholeness.

PREVIOUS PUBLISHING CREDITS

"Beloved" was first published in *Scintilla* journal issue 23.

"Lost" was published on the Pendemic.ie website.

"First Kiss," "Autobiography," "So Much is Ending," "Ludwig," "Letter to My Adolescent Self," "Origins," "Dreams," "I Want to Be the Kind of Woman," and "Where has the wild woman gone?" were published on the *Impspired* website.

"At the End of Time" was published in *Spiritus Journal.*

"Suspended" was first shared on the *Holy Shenanigans* podcast.

"Field Notes of an Orphan" won first place in the Bangor Poetry Competition and was published in the *Bangor Journal.*

"After My Grandmother Died" was published in *Vita Poetica.*

"Waxing and Waning" was published in *Bearings.*

"Saint Francis," "Julian of Norwich in Her Sick Bed," "You Know Now," and "Migration" were all published in *U.S. Catholic* magazine.

IRON
PEN

> "O that my words were written down!
>
> O that they were inscribed in a book!
>
> O that with an iron pen and with lead
>
> they were engraved on a rock forever!"
>
> —Job 19:23–24

Outcast and utterly alone, Job pours out his anguish to his Maker. From the depths of his pain, he reveals a trust in God's goodness that is stronger than his despair, giving humanity some of the most beautiful and poetic verses of all time. Paraclete's Iron Pen imprint is inspired by this spirit of unvarnished honesty and tenacious hope.

OTHER IRON PEN BOOKS

ABOUT PARACLETE PRESS

Paraclete Press is the publishing arm of the Cape Cod Benedictine community, the Community of Jesus. Presenting a full expression of Christian belief and practice, we reflect the ecumenical charism of the Community and its dedication to sacred music, the fine arts, and the written word.

SCAN
TO
READ
MORE

YOU MAY ALSO BE INTERESTED IN . . .

DREAMING OF STONES

Poems

CHRISTINE VALTERS PAINTNER

www.paracletepress.com